JUL 2013

JUL 2013

Creatures of the Deep

GLASS SQUID

AND OTHER SPECTACULAR SQUID

Casey Rand

Raintree

Chicago, Illinois

www.heinemannraintree.com
Visit our website to find out
more information about
Heinemann-Raintree books.

To order:
☎ Phone 888-454-2279
💻 Visit www.heinemannraintree.com
to browse our catalog and order online.

©2012 Raintree
an imprint of Capstone Global Library, LLC
Chicago, Illinois

Edited by Megan Cotugno and Abby Colich
Designed by Philippa Jenkins
Illustratred by Terry Pastor / www.theartagency.co.uk
Picture research by Hannah Taylor
Originated by Capstone Global Library
Printed and bound in China by CTPS

15 14 13 12 11
10 9 8 7 6 5 4 3 2 1

Library of Congress Cataloging-in-Publication Data
Rand, Casey.
  Glass squid and other spectacular squid / Casey Rand.—1st ed.
      p. cm.—(Creatures of the deep)
  Includes bibliographical references and index.
  ISBN 978-1-4109-4194-7 (hc)—ISBN 978-1-4109-4201-2 (pb) 1. Squids—Juvenile literature. 2. Cranchiidae—Juvenile literature. I. Title.
  QL430.2.R36 2012
  594'.58—dc22   2010038186

Acknowledgments
We would like to thank the following for permission to reproduce photographs:

© Kevin Raskoff p. 20; © Seapics.com p. 14 (David Shen); Alamy Images p. 13 (© WaterFrame); Corbis pp. 17 (© Visuals Unlimited), 29 (© EPA/Christopher Berkey); FLPA pp. 9, 11 (Minden Pictures/ Norbert Wu), 10 (D P Wilson), 18 (Minden Pictures/ Fred Bavendam); Image courtesy of the Monterey Bay Aquarium Research Institute p. 23; Image Quest Marine p. 5; naturepl.com pp. 6, 15 (David Shale); Photolibrary pp. 4 (OSF/ Mark Deeble & Victoria Stone), 21 (OSF/ Mark Conlin), 27 bottom (Pacific Stock/ James Watt); Rex Features p. 24 (Newspix); Science Photo Library pp. 16 (Dante Fenolio), 22 (Alexis Rosenfeld); SeaPics.com pp. 12 (Bob Cranston), 19 (Mark Strickland); Shutterstock p. 27 top (© erwinova)

Cover photograph of Glass squid reproduced with permission of © Image Quest Marine.

We would like to thank Michael Bright for his invaluable help in the preparation of this book.

CONTENTS

Some words are printed in bold, **like this**. You can find out what they mean by looking in the glossary.

THE MYSTERIOUS DEEP SEA

Far below the surface of the ocean lies an entire world of unknown and mysterious **organisms** and animals. Many of these creatures have never been seen or studied by humans. In many ways, scientists know more about outer space than they do about what goes on deep in our own sea. The deep sea is Earth's final frontier, still waiting to be fully explored with many mysteries to be revealed.

Exploring the ocean

Deep in the sea there are enormous amounts of **pressure**, small amounts of light, and very cold temperatures. To explore these cold, dark, high-pressure areas, scientists must use special **chambers** made of steel, or other strong materials, to protect themselves.

Special vehicles are used to explore the deep sea.

Scientists estimate there are more than nine million **species** of animals yet to be discovered in the ocean.

Squid family

One of the most exciting animals that lives in the deep sea is the squid. There are over 300 amazing species, or types, of squid already discovered in the ocean. There are likely to be many more undiscovered species.

THE GLASS SQUID

The glass squid family includes more than 60 different **species** of squid. They have this name because, like glass, most are almost completely **transparent**! This helps them avoid **predators**, or animals that might want to eat them.

Creatures great and small

Glass squid range in size from very tiny to enormous. The piglet squid is only 100 millimeters (4 inches) long, while the colossal squid may reach 15 meters (almost 50 feet)! Despite their differences, they are both members of the glass squid family and are closely related.

The piglet squid is one of the smallest known glass squid.

100 millimeters (4 inches)

Ocean Zones

Scientists divide the ocean into five zones. These zones include the water's surface and the ocean floor. Glass squid can be found from the sunlight zone down to the cold, dark abyssal zone.

0 meters
200 meters (700 feet)
Sunlight Zone
Twilight Zone
1,000 meters (3,300 feet)
Midnight Zone
4,000 meters (13,100 feet)
Abyssal Zone
6,000 meters (19,700 feet)
Earth/Rock
Hadal Zone
Earth/Rock
11,000 meters (36,100 feet)

Home of the glass squid

Glass squid live in salt water throughout the world's oceans. Some glass squid stay deep below the ocean's surface, but others live near the surface.

SQUID PARTS

Did you know squid have three hearts? Squid have two small hearts for pumping blood to their **gills**, the structures through which they breathe. They also have one larger heart for pumping blood to the rest of their body.

Squid smarts

Squid are some of the most intelligent **invertebrates**, or animals without backbones. Squid have a large head made of **cartilage**, like the material in your ears, which holds a large brain.

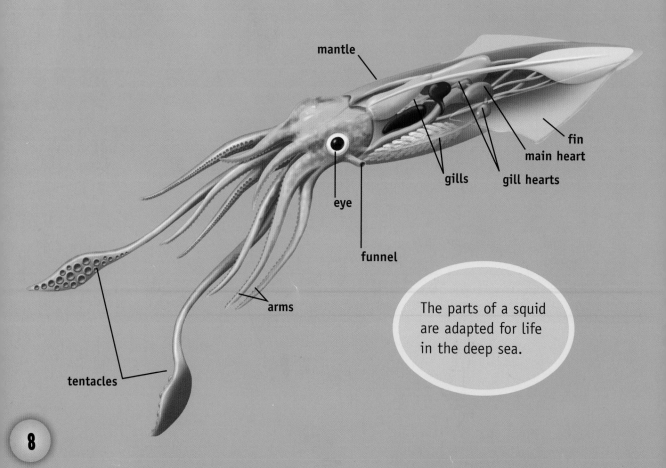

mantle

fin

main heart

gills

gill hearts

eye

funnel

arms

tentacles

The parts of a squid are adapted for life in the deep sea.

Squid vs. Octopus

The squid and octopus families are similar, but not the same.

Characteristic	Squid	Octopus
Size	more than 20 meters (66 feet)	less than 5 meters (16 feet)
Arms	8 arms and 2 tentacles	8 arms
Suckers	suction cups with hooks (usually)	suction cups
Fins	2 fins	none (usually)

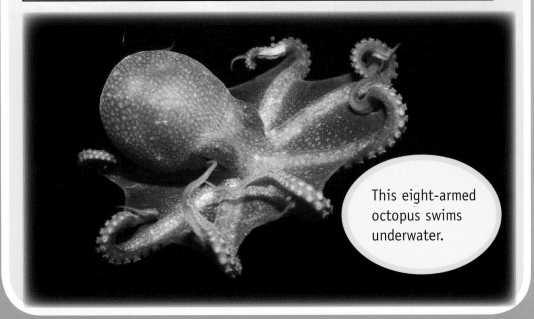

This eight-armed octopus swims underwater.

Fit for sea

The body of the squid is built to survive the deep sea. The squid does not have bones. Bones could be crushed by the enormous **pressure** of the deep sea. Squid muscles contain a liquid called **ammonia**. Ammonia is lighter than water. This helps the squid move easily through water.

THE SQUID LIFE

An average squid lives anywhere from one to two years. They usually live in the same area for most of their lives. However, they generally **migrate** before **reproducing**.

Squid love

There are male and female squid, and reproduction takes place by mating. Many types of squid travel alone, but during mating season they swarm together into large groups. Female squid can carry as many as 10 million eggs. Once the eggs are **fertilized**, the female will attach them to a rock or leave them in a safe area. Squid die after they reproduce.

Adult squid swarm together during mating season.

Squid eggs are placed in a safe place and left to grow alone.

Baby squid

When baby squid hatch from their eggs, they may appear to be tiny versions of adult squid. Since adult squid die after reproducing, baby squid must survive on their own. These mini squid stay near the surface of the water where they feed on **plankton** and grow stronger. As they grow, squid move farther and farther below the surface of the water.

FLYING SQUID

Squid are the fastest moving **invertebrates** in the ocean. The Humboldt squid is known as the jumbo flying squid. It can swim 25 kilometers (16 miles) per hour! It sometimes swims so fast to avoid **predators** that it throws itself out of the water—flying a short distance in the air.

This Humboldt squid was found in the waters surrounding Mexico.

Underwater jet propulsion

Squid have a unique way of swimming. A squid sucks water into a muscular **cavity** called a **mantle** cavity. The squid then rapidly **contracts** the cavity, shooting the water out through a funnel. This propels, or moves, its body through the water. The squid's funnel can be aimed in any direction, so the squid can swim any way it chooses.

Pack attack

The Humboldt squid can grow to over 1.8 meters (6 feet) long and weigh up to 45 kilograms (100 pounds). Like all squid, they are carnivores, or meat-eaters. Humboldt squid hunt in schools of up to 1,200. They are very aggressive and will even eat each other if other food is difficult to find.

This Humboldt squid is eating a member of the same **species**!

THE HUNTERS AND THE HUNTED

Squid hunt many other animals for food, but are also hunted by many animals. Fortunately for squid, they are talented hunters. They are also talented at escaping other **predators**.

Hunters

Squid are carnivores that hunt fish, shrimp, crabs, other squid, and many other underwater animals. Many squid hunt by staying very still and waiting for food to get close enough to grab.

The goblin shark is a predator of squid.

Squid have a bird-like beak used for tearing into their prey.

Beak

Tools of the hunt

Most squid have two long tentacles. The ends are covered in suction cups and hooks. These are used for grabbing **prey**. These tentacles also have sensors that tell the squid whether the prey will taste good or bad. The tentacles pass captured food to the squid's eight arms, which pull the prey in to be eaten.

Hunted

Squid are hunted by many deep-sea creatures such as goblin sharks, whales, and eels. Even the biggest squid, those nearly 15 meters (49 feet) long, are eaten by the sperm whale, which may grow up to 19 meters (62 feet) long.

DISAPPEARING ACT

Squid have amazing talents for escaping **predators**. Many glass squid are clear. This makes them very difficult to see. Some other types of squid can nearly disappear to avoid predators!

Squid lights

Certain squid, such as the firefly squid, have **photophores**. Photophores are special cells that can produce light, just like a flashlight. Squid can use this light to make their shadow disappear. Or the squid can use a flash of bright light to temporarily blind a predator, giving the squid time to escape.

The firefly squid can make its own light.

Can Squid Ink Cure Disease?

Recently, scientists have found that squid ink is toxic to certain types of cancer cells. There is more research to do, but squid ink may help cure diseases one day.

Ink cannon

Most squid produce and store a dark ink. A squid can shoot this ink into the water and disappear before predators realize what happened.

Squid ink contains **melanin**, the same substance that gives your skin its color.

CAMOUFLAGE SQUID

The Caribbean Reef Squid can change color to blend in with almost any environment. This is known as camouflage, but unlike camouflage pants, these squid can quickly change colors! Camouflage helps the Reef Squid hide from **predators** and sneak up on **prey**.

Coat of many colors

Chromatophores are cells in the skin of the Reef Squid. Each chromatophore has a certain color. These are similar to the cells that make your eyes look blue, green, hazel, or brown. But the squid has many different colored chromatophores. This allows the squid to rapidly change from green to blue.

Reef Squid can change color and pattern to disappear into the background.

Reef Squid can use each side of their body to send a different message at the same time!

Color communication

Squid can use color changes to communicate with each other. They send messages to other squid by changing color, showing patterns of color, and by flashing certain colors. In fact, some squid can send two different messages to different squid at the same time.

EXPLORING THE DEEP SEA

There are thousands of deep-sea animals that scientists know very little about, and thousands of others that remain undiscovered. To learn about these creatures, scientists have to find a way to explore the deepest parts of the ocean.

This rarely photographed deep-sea creature is a type of octopus.

The Aquarius Reef Base allows study of the underwater world.

Danger in the deep sea

The deep sea is filled with danger. The water in the deep sea has very little oxygen and very low temperatures. Even more dangerous are the high **pressure** levels found there. Water presses down on everything below it. Deep in the sea, there is a lot of water pushing down from above, creating high pressure. This makes exploring the deep sea very difficult.

Astronauts of the sea

To study the deep sea, scientists use special equipment that can handle the pressure and cold temperatures. Some scientists work in a special underwater laboratory to study sea life. The scientists who work there are known as **aquanauts**. They can stay underwater for weeks at a time in the laboratory.

ALIEN SQUID

The development of sea laboratories and **submersibles** (small vehicles built to explore underwater) has led to the discovery of many mysterious sea creatures. Some of the most amazing are a group of large, interesting squid that scientists are now beginning to learn about.

Alien encounter

In 1988 the crew of a manned submersible called *Nautile* made a remarkable discovery. Over 4,500 meters (15,000 feet) deep they spotted a huge squid with very long arms. The squid was unlike any that anyone had ever seen. This squid has since been named the long-armed squid.

Nautile is a manned submersible used to search the deep sea.

This mysterious squid with arms 10 meters (33 feet) long was seen lurking in the Gulf of Mexico.

Long-armed squid

Since the first sighting of the long-armed squid, several of these squid have been spotted by submersibles. However, scientists have not been able to capture and study any adult long-armed squid. We know that these squid have large fins, large eyes, and extremely long arms. Otherwise, these squid remain mysterious— almost completely unknown to humans.

MONSTERS OF THE SEA

Deep below the surface of the sea live monstrous squid even larger than the long-armed squid. These squid stay hidden in the deepest, darkest parts of the ocean. We know very little about them.

Giant squid

The first discovery of a giant squid occurred 900 meters (2,950 feet) deep in the ocean. The largest giant squid ever found was 18 meters (59 feet) long. They have eyes as large as basketballs! The giant squid is only the second largest of the squid. Scientists have discovered another even larger squid named the colossal squid. It is the largest known **invertebrate** on Earth.

This 227 kilogram (500 pound) giant squid was found dead off the coast of Australia.

Giant killer

While these giant squid are near the top of the **food chain**, they are hunted by an even bigger animal—the humongous sperm whale. The beaks of giant squid are often found in the bellies of sperm whales. Some whales even have scars from doing battle with giant squid.

Squid Sizes

Semi-trailer Truck
18 meters (60 feet)

Sperm Whale
20 meters (66 feet)

Humboldt Squid
2 meters (6.6 feet)

Giant Squid
13 meters (43 feet)

Colossal Squid
14 meters (46 feet)

0   5   10   METERS   15   20   25

MAN VS. SQUID

Squid are known to be aggressive and skilled hunters. But do squid ever attack humans or ships?

Tales from the sea

For centuries sailors have told stories of giant creatures in the dark waters of the sea. After World War II, survivors of some sunken ships told stories of men being pulled from ships and eaten by giant squid-like monsters. But none of these stories have been officially verified. It remains a mystery whether giant squid could really attack a ship.

Fishing for squid

Fisheries are businesses that raise or catch underwater animals to sell, usually for food. While some squid are eaten by humans, most deep-sea squid are not. These squid have packets of **ammonia** that make them taste very bad to humans. However, deep-sea squid hunt some of the same fish that fisheries catch. This may make it more difficult for these squid to find enough food.

Some squid are eaten by humans, but most deep-sea squid would not taste good.

Overfishing an area may change the **food chain**.

SQUID IN DANGER

While deep-sea squid are not fished by humans for food, the activities of humans can affect all life in the oceans, including deep-sea squid.

Harmful emissions

Scientists believe CO_2 **emissions** are causing a decrease in oxygen levels in ocean water. This may cause some squid, such as the Humboldt squid, to become less active, and thus more likely to be eaten by **predators**. This could significantly affect the **food chain** and is a major concern for scientists.

Spilled oil

In 2010 an oil well in the Gulf of Mexico was damaged and began spilling oil into the sea. Oil is known to be poisonous to almost all life-forms. While deep-sea squid may not come into direct contact with this oil, **plumes** of oil deep underwater may harm them. And many of the fish, shrimp, and other animals that squid hunt are harmed by oil spills. This could cause a dangerous shortage of food for deep-sea squid.

Floating oil can be extremely dangerous to sea life.

GLOSSARY

ammonia colorless, smelly substance that is lighter than water

aquanauts name for scientists who work in laboratories in the ocean

cartilage elastic-like connective tissue found in various parts of the body, such as the joints

cavity unfilled space in a mass, such as a rock

chamber room

chromatophore cell that contains a colored pigment and can, by expansion or contraction, change the color of the skin

CO_2 emissions carbon dioxide gas that has been released into the air

contract squeeze or force together

fertilize begin reproduction

fishery place where fish or other aquatic animals are caught to be sold

food chain chain of animals and organisms in a region that rely on each other for energy from food

gill organ through which a fish or underwater animal breathes

invertebrate animal that does not have a backbone or spinal column

mantle main body of the squid that holds the brain, lungs, heart, and other organs

melanin substance that gives skin its color

migrate move from one place to another

organism living thing

photophore light-producing organ found especially in underwater animals

plankton collection of small or microscopic organisms that float or drift in fresh or salt water, especially at or near the surface

plume column or band of a substance

predator organism that lives by capturing and eating other organisms

pressure force pressed on something

prey animal hunted or caught for food

reproduce to have babies

species category or kind of animal that shares the same name

submersible vessel capable of operating or remaining underwater

transparent something that is clear or can be seen through

FIND OUT MORE

Books

Coldiron, Deborah. *Squid (Underwater World)*. Edina, Minn.: ABDO, 2007.

Markle, Sandra. *Outside and Inside Giant Squid (Outside and Inside)*. New York: Walker Books for Young Readers, 2005.

Rhodes, Mary Jo. *Octopuses and Squid (Undersea Encounters)*. Danbury, Conn.: Children's Press, 2006.

Websites

http://dsc.discovery.com/news/2008/05/01/colossal-squid.html
This slide show examines a colossal squid that was caught in New Zealand.

www.thecephalopodpage.org/
Visit this site to read about the cephalopod group, which includes squid.

http://animals.nationalgeographic.com/animals/invertebrates/giant-squid/
Learn more information about the giant squid.

INDEX